OUR
FEATURE
PRESENTATION:

MANAGEMENT

JOSEPH E. CHAMPOUX
THE ROBERT O. ANDERSON SCHOOLS OF MANAGEMENT
THE UNIVERSITY OF NEW MEXICO

THOMSON
SOUTH-WESTERN

Australia · Canada · Mexico · Singapore · Spain · United Kingdom · United States

THOMSON

SOUTH-WESTERN

Our Feature Presentation: Management, 1e

by

Joseph E. Champoux, Ph.D.

Vice President /Editorial Director:
Jack W. Calhoun

Vice President/ Editor-in-Chief:
Michael P. Roche

Senior Publisher:
Melissa S. Acuña

Executive Editor:
John Szilagyi

Sr. Developmental Editor:
Judith O'Neill

Sr. Marketing Manager:
Rob Bloom

Sr. Media Technology Editor:
Vicky True

Media Developmental Editor:
Kristen Meere

Media Production Editor:
Karen L. Schaffer

Production Editor:
Daniel C. Plofchan

Editorial Assistant:
Molly Flynn

Manufacturing Coordinator:
Rhonda Utley

Printer:
Webcom, Ltd.; Toronto, ON

Sr. Design Project Manager:
Mike Stratton

Cover Designer:
Mike Stratton

Cover Photograph/Illustration:
©PhotoDisc, Inc.

Library of Congress Publishing Catalog
Control Number: 2003108303

Package ISBN: 0-324-28281-8

Book ISBN: 0-324-22219-X

Access Card ISBN: 0-324-22216-5

To my daughter Nicole. If you had not watched Top Gun *in our living room many years ago, this project would have never happened.*

P r e f a c e

South-Western, a division of Thomson Learning, proudly presents *Our Feature Presentation: Management*. This collection of twenty film scenes shows many management principles, theories, and concepts. Designed as a student workbook to accompany the third edition of Chuck Williams' *Management*, or any other principles of management textbook from South-Western, it will help you learn management principles and concepts through the magic and power of film.

This book is the product of my on-going cinema-based research and cinema-based teaching. I have found that students respond positively to the link between film scenes and abstract theories and concepts. Film offers a visualization of management concepts that often are abstract in textbooks and lectures. For example, one can read about ethical dilemmas. A visualization of ethical dilemmas with a carefully chosen film scene can reinforce it dramatically. *Emperor's Club* (2002) has a closing scene showing an ethical dilemma. Mr. Hundert (Kevin Kline), a preparatory school professor, discusses the value of principled living with former student Sedgewick Bell (Joel Gretsch). Sedgewick's reaction might surprise you. Or is it a common modern reaction to questions of ethical behavior?

This book has two parts. Part I, "Film as a Learning Resource," describes the unique aspects of film that make it a powerful learning resource. Read this part first before beginning to use film in your learning program.

Part II, "Film Scenes for Learning Management Principles, Theories, and Concepts" has film and scene descriptions for twenty topics. I present the film scene for each topic in a convenient two-page format. The first page describes the film and the scene; the second page has space for your name, your analysis, and personal reactions.

Each scene discussion includes film and scene descriptions, and a list of questions and issues to think about and watch for while viewing the scene. There is also a list of concepts or examples. If these concepts or examples appear in the scene, you can check them off when you see them. Marking them as you see them helps you write your analysis.

You can use this book in different ways. Your instructor might show the scene in class for class discussion. Or, your instructor may assign scenes for your out-of-class viewing as an individual or in small groups. He or she may want you to write your analysis and turn it in for class credit.

You can also use film scenes in this book for individual or group presentations in other classes. For example, the operations management and control scenes (Scenes 16 and 7) will work well in presentations for an Operations Management class. Using film scenes in such presentations can enliven them and help you make your points effectively.

This book also works well for independent study. All film scenes described in this book are available to you on-line. The Part II introduction gives you complete access instructions. You can supplement your reading and other studying by viewing scenes linked to topics you are trying to learn.

I based the film descriptions in this book on the latest versions of the following film reference sources:

- *Leonard Maltin's Movie & Video Guide*
- *The Seventh Virgin Film Guide*
- *VideoHound's DVD Guide, Books 1–3*
- *VideoHound's Golden Movie Retriever*

I also used the Internet Movie Database (*http://www.imdb.com*) and different film studies resources referenced throughout this book.

You may enjoy learning more about a specific film. I suggest using the reference books mentioned and the Internet Movie Database. This site has news about new and older films and lets you search for specific film information. It also has message boards where you can chat with other people about films.

The Web site *http://champoux.swlearning.com* has helpful documents such as "Cinema Resources on the World Wide Web," an extensive collection of useful and fun cinema Web sites. I will regularly update this site to include other helpful sources for learning with film. The site also will have updates for the films in *Our Feature Presentation: Management*. Descriptions of new film scenes that complement this book are also available to enhance your learning.

Many people helped bring this project to successful completion. Months of dedicated work identified scenes, edited scenes, and licensed the talent that appears in the scenes. Each actor or actress in the scenes signed a licensing agreement so we could bring these scenes to you. This complex collection of activities was in the capable hands of the "Magnificent Four" at Corbis Corporation.

My thanks go to Gary Shenk, leader of the Magnificent Four; Curtis Bowden, Senior Project Manager; licensing wizard Diane Rabideau; and Amy Katnik, Project Coordinator who informed me of licensing status with weekly reports. Job well done! Merci beaucoup!

I also thank Dan Plofchan, my production editor at South-Western, for keeping me well focused. Special thanks go to John Szilagyi, my executive editor, for conceiving and launching this project—the only one of its kind in the world. I also thank Kendra Robin, a Summer 2003 undergraduate student at The Robert O. Anderson School of Management, for her help with my observations on *Dr. Seuss' How the Grinch Stole Christmas*.

An effort such as this workbook is always a "work-in-progress." Please send me feedback about any aspect of its content and design. Send your comments and observations to me at The Robert O. Anderson Schools of Management, MSC05 3090, 1 University of New Mexico, Albuquerque, New Mexico, 87131-0001 USA. You can also send e-mail to *champoux@unm.edu*.

Joseph E. Champoux
Albuquerque, New Mexico, USA

C o n t e n t s

Film as a Learning Resource*

Videotaped films are now widely available for inexpensive rental or purchase, making them an accessible learning resource. Films now available from a video store include contemporary films, classical films, foreign films, documentaries, and some television series. About 24,000 such films are available on videotape, laserdisc, and DVD (Craddock 2002; Maltin 2002; Martin and Porter 2002).

Film scenes offer a visual portrayal of abstract theories and concepts discussed in typical management textbooks and taught in related courses. Viewing concepts through different film scenes also shows the application of these concepts in different situations.

I refer to specific film scenes at several points as examples of the observation discussed. The source article in the footnote for this summary discusses those scenes in more detail.

Film Theory

A review of the film theory and the film studies literature suggested some unique features of film that make it an uncommonly powerful learning tool. An early film theorist, Siegfried Kracauer, captured this view of film when he said: "[A unique property of film is its ability to] make one see and grasp things which only the cinema is privileged to communicate" (Kracauer 1973, x).

Some unique aspects of film and film making let this medium show management principles and concepts in an uncommonly powerful way. Understanding these aspects of film will help you understand the examples of scenes discussed later and throughout this book.

---

* *Source:* Adapted from Joseph E. Champoux, "Film as a Teaching Resource." *Journal of Management Inquiry*, Vol. 8, No. 2 (June 1999): 206–217 © 1999 Sage Publications, Inc. Reprinted by permission of Sage Publications, Inc. See this article for a more detailed description and full citations for this summary on learning with film.

Film Characteristics

Film records physical reality but sees it differently from ordinary human experiences (Andrew 1984; Arnheim 1957). Film is unequaled in its ability to hold and direct the attention of the viewer. Lens techniques, focusing techniques, camera movements, camera angles, framing of shots, and film editing can create gripping views not found in reality (Carroll 1985). The following summarizes these major film characteristics.

- **Close-up shot**: Lets a director show a viewer something that might go unnoticed with ordinary vision. Example: *12 Angry Men*
- **Long shot**: Shows the viewer more than what ordinary vision shows. Example: *Broadcast News*
- **Deep focus**: All parts of a scene are in focus from the nearest object to the farthest. Example: *The Hudsucker Proxy*
- **Soft focus**: Keeps objects nearest the viewer in focus; puts objects farther away out of focus. Example: *Top Gun*
- **Film editing**: Puts a series of images together in a unique sequence intended to have specific effects on the viewer. Example: *The Godfather*
- **Shot/reverse-shot**: Shows social interaction between two or more parties; scene switches from a view of one party to a view of the other party in the conversation. Example: *Broadcast News*
- **Sound, dialogue**: Delivery of dialogue by the actor or actress adds to the drama, humor, or satire of a scene. Example: *Head Office*
- **Sound, composed music**: Deliberately controlled in tempo, loudness, and color to give desired effects to the cinematic experience. Example: *Top Gun*
- **Sound, music taken from other sources**: Often has meaning for viewers from earlier exposure to the music; lets a director use borrowed music as a satirical device or emphasize meaning to certain film themes. Example: *2001: A Space Odyssey*
- **Special effects**: Enhancements that come from many sources; computer effects are increasingly common in modern films. Example: *Metropolis*

Viewer Responses

Viewers are not passive observers of images on a screen. They can have many different responses, some of which come from film's unique features (Allbritton and Gerrig 1991; Gerrig and Prentice 1996). Viewer responses often become an essential part of the film experience.

The shot/reverse-shot editing technique described earlier creates a viewing experience that does not happen in the real world. A viewer can see all aspects of the conversation the director considers important to the film's story. Nonverbal cues from eye movement, facial expression, and body movement can load images with information a viewer interprets. Directors can embed these scenes with high emotional, satirical, or comical content that a viewer can only experience with the film medium.

Media, Cognition, and Learning

Traditional learning media include lecture/discussion and printed media such as book materials or projected text. Visual forms include overhead projection of drawings, slide projection of images, or computer projection of slides. I recommend adding film and film scenes to existing learning and instructional media. Several lines of research suggest different learning effects of different media forms. The conclusion from both brain and media and cognition research points compellingly to using multi-media for learning.

Learning Functions of Film

Films can serve many learning functions. The functions that will work for you depend on your learning style and learning goals. The following is an overview of ways of using film as case, metaphor, satire, symbolism, meaning, experience, and time.

- **Film as Case**: Case analysis is an obvious use of film and perhaps the first that one thinks of when considering film for learning. Scenes from a well-acted and well-directed film present material more dramatically and engagingly than a print case. Example: *The Coca-Cola Kid*
- **Film as Metaphor**: Metaphors serve many functions in prose and poetry and can serve similar functions when using film for learning (Cooper 1986; Hawkes 1972; Mooij 1976). Metaphors often leave lasting impressions that a person easily recalls. Example: *Scent of a Woman*
- **Film as Satire**: Satire is an effective art form for burning concepts into a person's mind (Feinberg 1967; Griffin 1994, 1; Test 1991). It uses humor and ridicule to contrast pretense and reality. Well-done satire can leave an unforgettable image of concepts you are trying to learn. Example: *Modern Times*
- **Film as Symbolism**: Some scenes from films can offer a symbolic way of communicating theories and concepts. Unusual shots, sequencing, lighting, and the use of black and white film often convey symbolism. Example: *Ikiru (to Live)*
- **Film as Meaning**: Film is an excellent medium for giving meaning to theories and concepts. The visual and auditory effects of great films can convey a message better than printed or spoken words. Example: *12 Angry Men*
- **Film as Experience**: The unique qualities of film described earlier can create strong experiences for viewers (Stadler 1990). You can use this feature of film to introduce yourself to other countries' cultures. Example: *Ciao, Professore!*

- **Film as Time**: Films portraying earlier periods can help show aspects of management and management behavior during an earlier time. Example: *Tucker: The Man and His Dream*

Ways of Using Film for Learning

There are several ways of using film for learning management principles, theories, and concepts (Proctor and Adler 1991; Zorn 1991). Experimenting with each method will show you which ones are most effective for your learning style and course content.

- **Before:** Viewing film scenes before reading or studying can give you a recallable visual image to which you can compare the topics you are studying. This approach allows quick reference to easily recallable examples shown in the film. Example: *Top Gun*
- **After:** Viewing scenes after reading or studying theories and concepts lets you use the scenes as a video case. This approach helps develop your analytical skills in applying what you are learning. Example: *Top Gun*
- **Repeat:** Repeating scenes is especially helpful when trying to develop your understanding of complex topics (Wolensky 1982). View the scenes before studying concepts to give you a visual anchor. Rerun the scenes to analyze them with the concepts you have studied. Example: *The Firm*
- **Comparison:** Films offer rich opportunities for comparisons in several ways. Remakes of the same film can offer a chance to see the same culture at different times. Example: *Sabrina* (1954); *Sabrina* (1995)

Summary

Film and film scenes are a widely available, easily accessed, learning resource. Many unique characteristics of film as a communication medium give it especially positive effects on learning. You can use film in different ways to enhance your learning: as case, metaphor, satire, symbolism, or experience. You also can align film scenes in different ways in your studying program. Try the film scenes in this book as enhancers for your study of management principles, concepts, and theories. You will surprise yourself about how much film can improve your learning and retention.

Film Scenes for Learning Management Principles, Theories, and Concepts

Part II has film descriptions, scene descriptions, discussion questions, and a list of concepts or examples for twenty management topics. Each scene appears in a convenient two-page format that lets you write your scene analysis on the second page. You also have space to include your personal reactions to the scene.

The film description summarizes the film's plot to help you understand the scene in the context of the entire film. Scene descriptions set the context of the scene within the film by describing what occurs before and after the scene. If you have not seen the film, or do not recall it easily, these descriptions will give you enough detail to understand the scene.

Some film scenes described in this book are either edited versions of the film's original scene or a composite of scenes from different parts of the film. If you have seen any of these films, do not be surprised if you cannot recall the exact scene presented to you. The scene descriptions tell you whether a scene was edited from the original or compiled from multiple scenes in the same film.

You can view the film scenes on the Internet by going to:

http://featurepresentation.swlearning.com

This URL takes you to the registration page for this film scene collection. You register once using the serial number that comes with this book. After registering on your first visit, you can return to view scenes by logging in with your username and password.

Your instructor has the same film scenes on either a VHS videotape or a CD-ROM. She or he can show the scenes during regular class meetings or might ask you to view them as an outside assignment.

You can view trailers for the films included in this book by going to:

http://www.imdb.com

Search for the film's title. You will then see a link that reads "(view trailer)." Turn on your computer's speakers and enjoy a brief overview given by the film's trailer. Watching the trailer can refresh your memory of a film you have seen or give you a useful overview of a film you have not seen.

8 Mile

Color, 2002
Running Time: 1 hour, 51 minutes
Rating: R
Director: Curtis Hanson
Distributor: *Universal Studios Home Video*

Jimmy "B-Rabbit" Smith Jr. (Eminem) wants success as a rapper and to prove that a white man can create some moving sounds. His job at the North Detroit Stamping plant fills his days while he pursues his music at night and sometimes on the plant's grounds. The film's title refers to Detroit's northern city boundary, well known to local people. This film gives a gritty look at 1995 Detroit's hip-hop culture and Jimmy's desires for acceptance by it. Eminem's original songs "Lose Yourself" and "8 Mile" received 2003 Golden Globe and Academy Award nominations. "Lose Yourself" won the Academy award for best original song. See Hanson (2002) for a film review and more details about *8 Mile*.

Scene: Working at North Detroit Stamping

This scene is an edited composite of two brief North Detroit Stamping sequences in *8 Mile*. The first half of the scene appears early in the film as part of "The Franchise" sequence. This scene's second half appears in the last 25 minutes of the film as part of the "Papa Doc Payback" sequence. Jimmy rides the city bus to work after his car fails to start and arrives for work late in the first part of this scene. The second part occurs after his beating by Papa Doc (Anthony Mackie) and Papa Doc's gang. Jimmy's mother (Kim Bassinger) returns to their trailer and tells him she won $3,200 at bingo. The film continues to its end and Jimmy's last battle (rapper competition).

What to Watch for and Ask Yourself

- What is your perception of the quality of Jimmy's job and his work environment?
- What is the quality of Jimmy's relationship with his foreman Manny (Paul Bates)? Does it change? If *yes*, why?
- How would you react to this type of work experience?

Concepts or Examples

☐ Working   ☐ Noise

☐ Work environment   ☐ Coworkers

☐ Supervisory behavior   ☐ Attention to work

☐ Workplace safety   ☐ Repetitive work

Analysis

_____

_____

_____

_____

_____

_____

Personal Reactions

_____

_____

_____

_____

_____

Blue Crush

Color, 2002
Running Time: 1 hour, 44 minutes
Rating: PG-13
Director: John Stockwell
Distributor: *Universal Studios Home Video*

Anne Marie Chadwick (Kate Bosworth) and her friends Eden (Michelle Rodriguez) and Lena (Sanoe Lake) work as hotel maids to support their commitment to surfing the magnificent waves of Hawaii's North Shore. They live in a simple beach shack where Anne Marie also cares for her sister Penny (Mika Boorem) Anne Marie trains daily to compete in the Pipe Masters surf competition. She also must fight off nagging fears from a near death surfing accident. Professional quarterback Matt Tollman (Matthew Davis) asks her to teach him to surf and their romance unfolds as an added distraction. *Blue Crush* is an easy film to watch with some extraordinary surfing sequences, including many with professional surfers.

Scene: No Fear

This scene occurs during the Pipe Masters competition on the North Shore of Oahu, Hawaii. It comes from the "No Fear" sequence near the end of the film. Anne Marie's first ride tossed her off her board and almost recreated her earlier accident. The judges gave her a score of 4.6, enough to move her into this second round. She now competes against top surfer Keala Kennelly (Herself). Anne Marie has not yet had a scoring ride in the second round. Kennelly has more points than Ann Marie but encourages and coaches her to catch a wave and have no fear. This section of the scene follows Kennelly's further encouragement to successfully ride "The Pipe."

What to Watch for and Ask Yourself

- What type of organizational environment does this scene symbolize? Stable, changeable, simple, complex?
- Does this environment hold certainty or uncertainty for those who interact with it?
- What parallels do you see between Anne Marie's interaction in this environment and a modern manager's interaction in a similar environment? What should managers do when faced with an environment of this type?

Concepts or Examples

☐ Environmental turbulence   ☐ Unstable environment

☐ Stable environment   ☐ Dynamic environment

☐ Turbulent environment   ☐ Changing environment

☐ Simple environment   ☐ Complex environment

Analysis

_____

_____

_____

_____

_____

Personal Reactions

_____

_____

_____

_____

Backdraft

Color, 1991
Running Time: 2 hours, 15 minutes
Rating: R
Director: Ron Howard
Distributor: *Universal Studios Home Video*

Two brothers follow their legendary late father's footsteps as a Chicago fire-fighter and join the force. Stephen "Bull" McCaffrey (Kurt Russell), the oldest, joins first and rises to the rank of Lieutenant. Younger brother Brian (William Baldwin) joins later and becomes a member of his older brother's Company 17. Sibling rivalry tarnishes their work relationships but they continue to successfully fight Chicago fires. Add a plot element about an adept mysterious arsonist and you have the basis of an ordinary film. The intense, unprecedented fire special effects give the viewer an unparalleled experience, short of participating in a fire fight. Chicago firefighters applauded the realism of the fire scenes (Craddock 2002, 79).

Scene: The First Day

This scene appears early in the film as part of "The First Day" sequence. Brian McCaffrey graduated from the fire academy and the Chicago fire department assigns him to his brother's company. This scene shows him fighting his first real fire at a garment factory. The film continues with Company 17 fighting the fire and Brian receiving some harsh first day lessons.

What to Watch for and Ask Yourself

- What parts of the Chicago fire department culture does this scene show? Does the scene show any cultural artifacts or symbols? If *yes*, what are they?
- Does the scene show any values that guide the firefighter's behavior?
- What does Brian McCaffrey learn on his first work day?

Concepts or Examples

☐ Cultural artifacts   ☐ Required behavior

☐ Values   ☐ Espoused values

☐ Norms   ☐ In-use values

☐ Cultural symbolism

Analysis

_____

_____

_____

_____

_____

Personal Reactions

_____

_____

_____

_____

_____

Emperor's Club

Color, 2002
Running Time: 1 hour, 49 minutes
Rating: PG-13
Director: Michael Hoffman
Distributor: *Universal Studios Home Video*

Principled and traditional Saint Benedict's Academy for Boys professor William Hundert (Kevin Kline) believes in teaching his students about living a principled life while teaching them his beloved classics. New student, young Sedgewick Bell's (Emile Hirsch) behavior challenges Hundert's principled ways. Bell's behavior during the 73rd annual competition of the Mr. Julius Caesar Contest suggests to Hundert that Bell leads a less than principled life, a point reinforced years later during a repeat of the competition.

Scene: Ethics Discussion

Mr. Hundert is the honored guest of his former student Sedgewick Bell (Joel Gretsch) at Bell's estate. Depaak Mehta (Rahul Khanna), Sedgewick, and Louis Masoudi (Patrick Dempsey) compete in a reenactment of the Mr. Julius Caesar competition. Bell wins the competition during which Mr. Hundert notices Bell's earpiece. Earlier in the film Mr. Hundert suspected that younger Segewick Bell wore an earpiece during the same event but Headmaster Woodbridge (Edward Herrmann) pressed him to ignore his suspicion.

This scene appears at the end of the film. It is an edited portion of the competition rematch sequence. Sedgewick announced his candidacy for the U.S. Senate just before talking to Mr. Hundert in the bathroom. In his announcement, he carefully described his commitment to specific values that he would pursue if he is elected.

What to Watch for and Ask Yourself

- Does Mr. Hundert describe a specific quality of life that one should lead? What are its elements?
- Does Sedgewick Bell lead that type of life? Is he committed to any specific ethical view or theory?
- What consequences or effects do you predict for Sedgewick Bell because of the way he chooses to live his life?

Concepts or Examples

☐ Ethics   ☐ Cheating

☐ Ethical behavior   ☐ Unethical behavior

☐ Ethical dilemma   ☐ Ethical view or theory

Analysis

_____

_____

_____

_____

_____

Personal Reactions

_____

_____

_____

_____

_____

Lorenzo's Oil

Color, 1992
Running Time: 2 hours, 15 minutes
Rating: PG-13
Director: George Miller
Distributor: *Universal Studios Home Video*

A true-life gripping story of young Lorenzo Odone[*], who suffers from an incurable degenerative brain disorder, ALD (adrenoleukodystrophy). Physicians and medical scientists offer little help to Lorenzo's desperate parents, Michaela (Susan Sarandon) and Augusto (Nick Nolte). They use their resources to learn about ALD to save their son. Director George Miller co-wrote the script that benefited from his medical training and experience as a physician.

Scene: The Symposium

Six months after Lorenzo's ALD diagnosis, his condition fails to improve with his restricted diet. Michaela and Augusto continue their research at the National Institutes of Health library, Bethesda, Maryland. Michaela finds a report of a critical Polish experiment that showed positive effects of fatty acid manipulation in rats. Convinced that a panel of experts could systematically focus on their problem, they help organize The First International ALD Symposium. This scene is an edited version of the symposium sequence that appears about midway in the film. The film continues with the Ordone's efforts to save their son.

What to Watch for and Ask Yourself

- Do the scientists present data or information during the symposium?
- If it is information, who transformed the data into information? Speculate about how such data becomes information.
- What do you predict is the next course of action for the Odone's?

---

[*] Six actors and actresses play Lorenzo throughout the film.

Concepts or Examples

☐ Information   ☐ Data transformation

☐ Data   ☐ Information processing

Analysis

_____

_____

_____

_____

_____

Personal Reactions

_____

_____

_____

_____

_____

Dr. Seuss' How the Grinch Stole Christmas*

Color, 2000
Running Time: 1 hour, 42 minutes
Rating: PG
Director: Ron Howard
Distributor: *Universal Studios Home Video*

Readers and lovers of the Dr. Seuss original tale might feel put off by Ron Howard's loose adaptation of the story.† Who-ville, a magical, mythical land, features two types of life: the Whos who love Christmas and the Grinch (Jim Carrey) who hates it. Cindy Lou Who (Taylor Momsen) tries to bring the Grinch back to the Yuletide celebrations, an effort that backfires for all involved. Sparkling special effects will dazzle most viewers and likely distract them from the film's departures from the original story.

Scene: Decisions, Decisions, Decisions

This scene is an edited version of the "Second Thoughts" sequence early in the film. Just before this scene, fearless Cindy Lou entered the Grinch's lair to invite him to be the Holiday Cheermeister at the Whobilation One-thousand celebration. In typical Grinch fashion, he pulls the trap door on Cindy Lou, who unceremoniously slides out of his lair to land on a snowy Who-ville street. The Grinch now must decide whether to accept the invitation. The film continues with the Cheermeister award ceremony.

What to Watch for and Ask Yourself

- What are the Grinch's decision alternatives or options?
- What decision criteria does the Grinch use to choose from the alternatives?
- Describe the steps in the Grinch's decision-making process.

---

* The film's short title is *How the Grinch Stole Christmas*.

† This film departs from Dr. Seuss' story almost immediately. The narrator's (Sir Anthony Hopkins) opening comments say, "Inside a snowflake, like the one on your sleeve, there happened s story you must see to believe." The narration then describes Who-ville, implying it exists inside a snowflake. All dedicated Whoists now that Who-ville exists inside a _____. (Answer on the next page.)

Concepts or Examples

☐ Decision-making process   ☐ Decision criteria

☐ Decision alternatives   ☐ Assess the decision

☐ Choice   ☐ Decision not to decide

Analysis

_____

_____

_____

_____

_____

Personal Reactions

_____

_____

_____

_____

_____

---

* Who-ville exists inside a speck of dust that Horton the elephant discovered floating through his jungle. See Dr. Seuss, *Horton Hears a Who!* New York: Random House, 1976.

Scent of a Woman

Color, 1992
Running Time: 2 hours, 37 minutes
Rating: R
Director: Martin Brest
Distributor: *MCA Universal Home Video*

Young Charlie Simms (Chris O'Donnell) tries to earn extra money over the Thanksgiving weekend for air fare to go home during his Christmas break. Ill-tempered, retired, and blind Lt. Colonel Frank Slade (Al Pacino) hires Charlie as his guide and caretaker for the weekend. Charlie, from Gresham, Oregon, is quiet, reserved, and has little experience with the opposite sex. He attends the exclusive Baird Preparatory School on a scholarship. His wild New York City weekend with Frank Slade bonds them forever. This film is a remake of *Profumo di Donna*, a 1974 Italian film.

Scene: The Ferrari

This scene follows Slade's morose moments in their hotel suite after the first day and night in Manhattan. Lt. Colonel Slade wants to sleep in and perhaps even die. Charlie convinces him to venture out on this beautiful day and go for a ride. They go to a Ferrari dealership where Slade convinces salesman Freddie Bisco (Leonard Gaines) to let a 17 year old driver and a blind man take the Ferrari Cabriolet T for a test drive. This scene appears in the last third of the film and defines the continued bonding of Frank Slade and Charlie Simms.

What to Watch for and Ask Yourself

- What pattern of control do these scenes show?
- What are the control system's elements?
- What type of performance measurement do these scenes show: periodic or continuous?

Concepts or Examples

- ☐ Control system
- ☐ Technology and control
- ☐ Feedback loop
- ☐ Performance standards
- ☐ Simple control

- ☐ Performance measurement
- ☐ Periodic monitoring
- ☐ Complex control
- ☐ Corrective action
- ☐ Continuous monitoring

Analysis

_____

_____

_____

_____

Personal Reactions

_____

_____

_____

_____

Mr. Baseball

Color, 1992
Running Time: 1 hour, 48 minutes
Rating: PG-13
Director: Fred Schepisi
Distributor: *MCA Universal Home Video*

The New York Yankees trade aging baseball player Jack Elliot (Tom Selleck) to the Chunichi Dragons, a Japanese team. This lighthearted comedy traces Elliot's bungling entry into Japanese culture where he almost loses everything, including his new girlfriend Hiroko Uchiyama (Aya Takanashi). He slowly begins to understand Japanese culture and Japanese baseball, ending with full acceptance by his teammates. This film has many examples of Japanese culture, especially its loving enthusiasm for baseball.

Scene: Meeting Hiroko's Family

Unknown to Hiroko's father, Jack and she have developed an intimate relationship. Unknown to Jack, Hiroko's father is "The Chief" (Ken Takakura), the Chunichi Dragons' manager. This scene follows the baseball game where "The Chief" removed Jack from the game. It shows Jack dining with Hiroko, her grandmother (Mineko Yorozuya), grandfather (Jun Hamamura), and father.

What to Watch for and Ask Yourself

- Does Jack Elliot behave as if he had cross-cultural training before arriving in Japan?
- Is he culturally sensitive or insensitive?
- What do you propose that Jack Elliot do for the rest of his time in Japan?

Concepts or Examples

☐ Cross-cultural experience   ☐ Cultural values

☐ Cross-cultural conflict   ☐ Entering a foreign culture

☐ Pre-departure training   ☐ Culture sensitivity

☐ Culture insensitivity

Analysis

_____

_____

_____

_____

_____

Personal Reactions

_____

_____

_____

_____

_____

The Bourne Identity

Color, 2002
Running Time: 1 hour, 59 minutes
Rating: PG-13
Director: Doug Liman
Distributor: *Universal Studios Home Video*

J ason Bourne (Matt Damon) cannot remember who he is but others believe he is an international assassin. Bourne tries to find his identity with the help of new friend and lover Marie (Franka Potente). While Bourne is discovering that he is an extremely well-trained and lethal agent, CIA agents pursue him across Europe to kill him. Loosely based on the Robert Ludlum 1981 novel. Previously filmed as a 1988 television miniseries starring Richard Chamberlain.

Scene: Bourne's Plan

This scene is an edited version of the "Bourne's Game" sequence near the end of the film. The day after Jason Bourne arrives at Eamon's (Tim Dutton) home with Marie, he kills the hired assassin who tried to kill him. Eamon is Marie's friend but a stranger to Jason. Jason uses the dead man's cellular telephone after returning to his Paris, France apartment. He presses the redial button, connecting him to Conklin (Chris Cooper), the CIA manager who is looking for him. Listen carefully to Jason's conversation with Conklin as he walks along the right bank of the river Seine in Paris.

What to Watch for and Ask Yourself

- Does Jason Bourne describe a plan to Conklin? If *yes*, what are the plan's elements? What is Bourne's goal?
- Does Bourne assess the plan's execution to conform to his goal? What does he do?
- Was Bourne's plan successfully carried out? Why or why not? How does this scene relate to organizational strategy and planning?

Concepts or Examples

☐ Planning

☐ Strategic planning

☐ Strategy

☐ Contingency planning

☐ Plan results

☐ Plan execution

☐ Environmental change

☐ Goal of a plan

Analysis

_____

_____

_____

_____

_____

Personal Reactions

_____

_____

_____

_____

Apollo 13 (I)

Color, 1995
Running time: 2 hours, 20 minutes
Rating: PG
Director: Ron Howard
Distributor: *MCA Universal Home Video*

This film dramatically portrays the flight of Apollo 13, the NASA mission to the moon that almost had an in-space disaster. Innovative problem solving and decision making amid massive ambiguity saved the crew. The film has many examples of both problem solving and decision making. Almost any set of scenes dramatically makes this point. Flight Director Gene Kranz wrote a book describing the Apollo 13 mission and the activities that prevented the in-space disaster (Kranz 2000).

A zero gravity simulator, a KC-135 four engine jet aircraft (NASA's "Vomit Comet"), helped create the film's realistic weightless scenes. These scenes required 600 parabolic loops over 10 days of filming (Craddock 2002, 66). See page 33 for a discussion of another scene from *Apollo 13*.

Scene: Carbon Dioxide Filter

This scene is a composite built from portions of the "CO2 Problem" sequence about 60 percent into the film and parts of the "With Every Breath ..." sequence that appears about 7 minutes later. The scene's first part follows the nearly complete shutdown of the Apollo 13 module to save battery power.

Mission Control detected rising CO2 levels in the module. The increasing CO2 levels could kill them if the NASA engineers cannot solve the problem on the ground. The film continues with the Apollo 13 crew building the carbon dioxide filter designed by the engineers.

What to Watch for and Ask Yourself

- What is the problem in this scene?
- What are the engineers' options for solving the problem?
- Does this scene show innovation and innovative behavior? If *yes*, in what form?

Concepts or Examples

☐ Problem solving   ☐ Decision making

☐ Problem identification   ☐ Innovation

☐ Options, alternatives   ☐ Innovative behavior

Analysis

_____

_____

_____

_____

_____

Personal Reactions

_____

_____

_____

_____

The Paper

Color, 1994
Running Time: 1 hour, 52 minutes
Rating: R
Director: Ron Howard
Distributor: *MCA Universal Home Video*

This engaging film shows the ethical dilemmas and stress of producing *The New York Sun*, a metropolitan daily newspaper. Metro Editor Henry Hackett (Michael Keaton) races against the clock to produce a story describing a major police scandal that could send two young Black men to jail. He is in constant conflict with his managing editor, Alicia Clark (Glenn Close), whose ambitions focus more on budget control than running accurate stories. Hackett also has constant pressure from his wife, Marty (Marisa Tomei), who is pregnant with their first child. She wishes he would take a less demanding job at *The Sentinel* and continually pushes for this while Hackett tries to get the story he wants.

Scene: Morning Staff Meeting

The day before this staff meeting, *The New York Sun* missed a story about murder and other shootings with racial overtones in New York City. Instead, *The Sun* ran a front-page story about parking problems. Senior Editor Bernie White (Robert Duvall) holds his regular morning staff meeting in which he discusses his preferences for front-page stories. This scene is an edited version of the "The Managing Editor" sequence early in *The Paper*.

What to Watch for and Ask Yourself

- Senior Editor Bernie White wants to reach a specific goal with the next edition of *The New York Sun*. What is the goal?
- What organizational form does this newspaper use? Is it organizational design by division, function, process, or matrix? Does *The Sun* departmentalize by product, customer, or geography?
- Is the organizational design of *The Sun* correct for reaching the goal? Why or why not?

Concepts or Examples

☐ Organizational structure

☐ Organizational design by function

☐ Process organizational design

☐ Departmentalization by geography

☐ Goals of organizational design

☐ Organizational design by project

☐ Matrix organizational design

☐ Departmentalization by customer

☐ Departmentalization by product

Analysis

_____

_____

_____

_____

_____

Personal Reactions

_____

_____

_____

_____

_____

The Breakfast Club

Color, 1985
Running Time: 1 hour, 32 minutes
Rating: R
Director: John Hughes
Distributor: *Universal Studios Home Video*

John Hughes' careful look at teenage culture in a Chicago suburban high school focuses on a group of teenagers from different subcultures of the school.[*] They start their Saturday detention with nothing in common, but over the course of a day, they learn each other's innermost secrets. This caring look at 1980's teenage culture leaves lasting impressions of its highly memorable characters: the Jock, the Princess, the Criminal, the Kook, and the Brain.[†]

Scene: Lunchtime

This scene lets you visit the high school detainees at lunchtime. It is an edited version of the "Lunchtime" sequence that appears in the first third of the film. Carefully study each character's behavior to answer the questions below.

What to Watch for and Ask Yourself

- Which *Big-Five* personality dimensions describe each character in this scene?
- Which characters show positive affectivity or negative affectivity?
- Are any of these characters a Type A personality or a Type B personality?

---

[*] Carson Shelton's passionate support for *The Breakfast Club* persuaded me to include a scene from this film in this collection.—J.E.C.

[†] If you have seen the film, try to recall which actor or actress played each character.

Concepts or Examples

☐ Individual differences
☐ Personality
☐ Type B personality
☐ Negative affectivity

☐ Type A personality
☐ Individual variability
☐ *Big-Five* personality dimensions
☐ Positive affectivity

Analysis

_____

_____

_____

_____

_____

_____

Personal Reactions

_____

_____

_____

_____

_____

Babe

Color, 1995
Running Time: 1 hour, 32 minutes
Rating: G
Director: Chris Noonan
Distributor: *Universal Studios Home Video*

A charming Australian film featuring eccentric, quiet Farmer Hoggett (James Cromwell) who trains a pig he won at the fair to herd his sheep. His eccentricity turns to determination when he enters the pig in the Australian National Sheepdog Championships. The Academy Award-winning visual effects include a seamless mixture of animatronic doubles, computer images, and live animals.

Scene: Herding Sheep

Farmer Hoggett's sheep dogs Rex (voiced by Hugo Weaving) and Fly (voiced by Miriam Margolyes), along with Babe (voiced by Christine Cavanaugh) the pig, accompany him to his sheep herd. Hogget needs to gather the sheep into a pen so he can sheer their wool. Before leaving for the pasture, Farmer Hoggett saw Babe carefully divide some chickens into two groups based on their color. Hoggett suspects that perhaps Babe might have some herding skills.

What to Watch for and Ask Yourself

- Are Babe's methods of herding sheep different from those used by the sheepdogs? If *yes*, what are the differences?
- Does Babe discover that he cannot successfully herd sheep as a sheep dog herds them? What does he do?
- Does Farmer Hoggett accept Babe for what he is—a pig not a sheep dog?

Concepts or Examples

☐ Diversity   ☐ Rejection of differences

☐ Different behaviors reach the same goal   ☐ Managing diversity

☐ Cannot change who you are   ☐ Valuing diversity

☐ Dimensions of diversity   ☐ Diversity and performance

      ☐ Acceptance of differences

Analysis

_____

_____

_____

_____

_____

Personal Reactions

_____

_____

_____

_____

Apollo 13 (II)

Color, 1995
Running time: 2 hours, 20 minutes
Rating: PG
Director: Ron Howard
Distributor: *MCA Universal Home Video*

This film recreates the heroic efforts of astronaut Jim Lovell (Tom Hanks), his crew, NASA, and Mission Control to bring their damaged Apollo spacecraft back to Earth. Examples of both problem solving and decision making occur in almost every scene. See page 25 for more information about this film and another scene discussion.

Scene: Bouncing Off the Walls

This scene appears during day 5 of the mission, about two-thirds into the film. Under instructions from mission control, astronaut Jack Swigert (Kevin Bacon) stirred the oxygen tanks early in Apollo 13's mission. An explosion in the spacecraft happened shortly after this procedure, causing unknown damage to the command module. Because of the damage, the crew has moved into the LEM (Lunar Exploration Module) , which becomes their lifeboat for the return to earth..

What to Watch for and Ask Yourself

- What triggers the conflict episode in these scenes?
- Is this intergroup conflict or intragroup conflict? What effects can such conflict have on the group dynamics on board Apollo 13?
- Does mission commander Jim Lovell successfully manage the group dynamics to return the group to a normal state?

Concepts or Examples

- ☐ Conflict
- ☐ Intragroup conflict
- ☐ Manifest conflict
- ☐ Group dynamics
- ☐ Interpersonal conflict

- ☐ Intergroup conflict
- ☐ Conflict episode
- ☐ Acceptance of differences
- ☐ Intrapersonal conflict
- ☐ Managing group dynamics

Analysis

_____

_____

_____

_____

_____

Personal Reactions

_____

_____

_____

_____

Bowfinger

Color, 1999
Running Time: 1 hour, 37 minutes
Rating: PG-13
Director: Frank Oz
Distributor: *Universal Studios Home Video*

This first-time combination of Steve Martin and Eddie Murphy's talents offers a funny look at a twist on Hollywood film making. Bobby Bowfinger (Martin), perhaps filmmaking's least successful director, wants to produce a low-budget film with top star Kit Ramsey (Murphy). Bowfinger's problem: recruit a crew and cast with almost no budget and trick Kit into appearing in his film.

Scene: The Lookalike

Bobbie Bowfinger interviews several candidates for the Kit Ramsey lookalike. He rejects all candidates until Jifferson (Jiff) Ramsey (Eddie Murphy) auditions. This scene is an edited version of the "The Lookalike" sequence early in the film. It includes Jiff's audition, interview, and a brief look at his first workday.

What to Watch for and Ask Yourself

- Does Bobbie Bowfinger have a set of valid selection criteria for filling the role of the Kit Ramsey lookalike? Does Bowfinger apply the criteria uniformly to each role applicant?
- Is there a good person-job fit of Jiff Ramsey in the screen role of Kit Ramsey?
- Do you predict Jiff Ramsey's success as a Kit Ramsey substitute?

Concepts or Examples

☐ Selection process

☐ Selection criteria

☐ Uniform application of selection criteria

☐ Selection criteria validity

☐ Job placement

☐ Person-job fit

Analysis

_____

_____

_____

_____

_____

Personal Reactions

_____

_____

_____

_____

Casino

Color, 1995
Running Time: 2 hours, 59 minutes
Rating: R
Director: Martin Scorcese
Distributor: *MCA Universal Home Video*

Martin Scorcese's lengthy, complex, and beautifully photographed *Casino* offers a close study of 1970's Las Vegas gambling casinos and their organized crime connections. It completes his trilogy that includes *Mean Streets* (1973) and the 1990 *Goodfellas* (Craddock 2002, 149). Ambition, greed, drugs, and sex ultimately destroy the mob's gambling empire. The film includes strong performances by Robert De Niro, Joe Pesci, and Sharon Stone. The violence and expletive-filled dialogue give *Casino* an R rating.

Scene: The Casino

This scene opens the film and establishes important background about casino operations. Listen carefully to Sam Rothstein's (Robert De Niro) voice-over. He quickly describes the casino's operation and how it tries to reach its goals. The scene comes from the beginning of "The Truth About Las Vegas" sequence in *Casino*.

What to Watch for and Ask Yourself

- What type of operation's management does this scene show? Manufacturing operations management or service operations management?
- Are customers directly involved in this operation? If *yes*, in what way? What likely effects do they have on the casino's operation and its management?
- Does the casino have independent or interdependent operation processes?

Concepts or Examples

☐ Operations management

☐ Interdependent process

☐ Customer participation

☐ Productivity management

☐ Service operations management

☐ Manufacturing operations management

☐ Independent process

Analysis

_____

_____

_____

_____

_____

_____

Personal Reactions

_____

_____

_____

_____

_____

For Love of the Game

Color, 1999
Running Time: 2 hours, 17 minutes
Rating: PG-13
Director: Sam Raimi
Distributor: *Universal Studios Home Video*

Billy Chapel (Kevin Costner), a twenty-year veteran pitcher for the Detroit Tigers, learns just before the season's last game that the new team's owners want to trade him. He also learns that his partner, Jane Aubrey (Kelly Preston), wants to leave him. Faced with these daunting blows, Chapel wants to pitch a perfect final game. Director Raimi's love of baseball shines through in some striking visual effects.

Scene: Just Throw

This scene is a slightly edited version of the "Just Throw" sequence. It is among the film's closing sequences as Chapel pitches his last game. Tiger's catcher Gus Sinski (John C. Reilly) comes out to the pitching mound to talk to Billy. This scene begins the film's exciting baseball game closing scenes.

What to Watch for and Ask Yourself

- What is Billy Chapel's level of esteem needs at this point in the game?
- Do you expect any effect on Chapel from Gus Sinski's talk? If *yes*, what is the effect?
- What rewards potentially exist for Billy Chapel? Remember, this is the last baseball game of his career.

Concepts or Examples

☐ Needs

☐ Esteem needs

☐ Self-esteem

☐ Motivation

☐ Performance

☐ Effort

☐ Self-actualization

☐ Rewards

Analysis

_____

_____

_____

_____

_____

_____

Personal Reactions

_____

_____

_____

_____

_____

U-571

Color, 2000
Running Time: 1 hour, 56 minutes
Rating: PG-13
Director: Jonathan Mostow
Distributor: *Universal Studios Home Video*

This World War II action-packed thriller involves a U.S. submarine crew's retrieval of an Enigma encryption device from a disabled German submarine. After the crew gets the device, the German's torpedo their submarine and it sinks. The survivors now must use the German submarine to escape from enemy destroyers. The almost non-stop action and extraordinary special effects look and sound best with a home theater system.

Scene: Submarine Commander

This scene is edited from the "To Be a Captain" sequence early in the film. The S33, an older U.S. submarine is underway on its secret mission. Before departure, the S33's officers received a briefing on their mission from Office of Naval Intelligence representatives on board. Executive Officer Lt. Andrew Tyler (Matthew McConaughey) reports on the submarine's status to Lt. Commander Mike Dahlgren (Bill Paxton). The film continues with the S33 finding the disabled German submarine.

What to Watch for and Ask Yourself

- What aspects of leadership does Lt. Commander Mike Dahlgren describe as important for a submarine commander?
- Which leadership behaviors or traits does he emphasize?
- Are these traits or behaviors right for this situation? Why or why not?

Concepts or Examples

☐ Leadership

☐ Management

☐ Leader behavior

☐ Leadership traits (self-confidence, dominance, task-relevant knowledge, etc.)

☐ Subordinate effects

☐ Follower effects

☐ Effective leadership

☐ Ineffective leadership

Analysis

_____

_____

_____

_____

_____

Personal Reactions

_____

_____

_____

_____

Patch Adams

Color, 1998
Running Time: 1 hour, 55 minutes
Rating: PG-13
Director: Tom Shadyac
Distributor: *Universal Studios Home Video*

Hunter "Patch" Adams (Robin Williams), a maverick medical student, believes laughter is the best medicine. The rest of the medical community believes that medicine is the best medicine. Patch Adams prefers closeness to his patients, not the aloofness of more traditional providers. Williams' wackiness comes through clearly in this film based on a true story.

Scene: Talking to the Meat Packers

This scene comes from the film's early sequence, "The Experiment," after the students' medical school orientation. Patch Adams and fellow medical student Truman Schiff (Daniel London) leave the University Diner. They begin Patch's experiment for changing the programmed responses of people they meet on the street. Along the way, they stumble upon a meat packer's convention where this scene occurs.

What to Watch for and Ask Yourself

- What parts of the communication process appear in this scene? Note each part of the process that you see in the scene.
- What type of communication does this scene show? Small group, large audience, or persuasive?
- Do you view Patch Adams as an effective communicator? Why or why not?

Concepts or Examples

- ☐ Communication process
- ☐ Sender(s)
- ☐ Receiver(s)
- ☐ Communication medium
- ☐ Encoding
- ☐ Message

- ☐ Large audience communication
- ☐ Persuasive communication
- ☐ Pair-wise communication
- ☐ Feedback
- ☐ Small group communication
- ☐ Communication effectiveness

Analysis

_____

_____

_____

_____

_____

Personal Reactions

_____

_____

_____

_____

_____

Back to the Future Part II

Color, 1989
Running Time: 1 hour, 48 minutes
Rating: PG
Director: Robert Zemeckis
Distributor: *Universal Studios Home Video*

Marty McFly (Michael J. Fox) and his girlfriend Jennifer (Elisabeth Shue) time travel to Hill Valley, California in the year 2015 with Dr. Emmett Brown (Christopher Lloyd). They want to help prevent their children from getting arrested for some allegedly illegal acts. While in the future, Marty buys a sports almanac for the years 1950 to 2000. He plans to make money from betting on games upon his return to his own time. Biff Tanen (Thomas F. Wilson) steals the almanac and the Delorean time machine with his own plans to return to 1985 to make money, build his power, and turn Hill Valley into a nightmarish community.

Scene: Looking Into the Future

This scene appears in the first thirty minutes of the film as part of the sequences "The Future McFlys" and "Chicken." Police returned previously unconscious Jennifer to the McFly's home because her thumbprint identified her as Jennifer Baker McFly. The scene shows McFly family interactions thirty years into the future.

What to Watch for and Ask Yourself

- Which technologies shown in these scenes exist today?
- Which technologies will exist in the future?
- Which technologies are still fantasies?

Concepts or Examples

☐ Future   ☐ Video conferencing

☐ Future technology   ☐ Video technology

☐ Telecommunication   ☐ Future management interaction

☐ Interaction

Analysis

_____

_____

_____

_____

_____

Personal Reactions

_____

_____

_____

_____

B i b l i o g r a p h y

Allbritton, D. W., and Gerrig, R. J. 1991. Participatory Responses in Prose Understanding. *Journal of Memory and Language* 30: 603–626.

Andrew, D. 1984. *Concepts in Film Theory*. New York: Oxford University Press, Inc.

Arnheim, R. 1957. *Film as Art*. Berkeley, CA: University of California Press.

Carroll, N. 1985. The Power of Movies. *Daedalus* 114: 79–103.

Cooper, D. E. 1986. *Metaphor*. Oxford, England: Basil Blackwell.

Craddock, J., ed. 2002. *VideoHound's Golden Movie Retriever*. Farmington Hills, MI: The Gale Group, Inc.

Feinberg, L. 1967. *Introduction to Satire*. Ames, IA: Iowa State University Press.

Gerrig, R. J., and Prentice, D. A. 1996. Notes on Audience Response. In *Post-Theory: Reconstructing Film Studies,* D. Bordwell and N. Carroll, eds., Ch. 18. Madison, WI: University of Wisconsin Press.

Griffin, D. 1994. *Satire: a Critical Reintroduction*. Lexington, KY: University Press of Kentucky.

Hanson, B. 2002. 8 Mile. *Primiere.com*. (http://www.premiere.com/article.asp?section_id=2&article_id=355&page_number=1) (October 15)

Hawkes, T. 1972. *Metaphor*. London: Methuen.

Kracauer, S. 1973. *Theory of Film: The Redemption of Physical Reality*. New York: Oxford University Press.

Kranz, G. 2000. *Failure Is Not an Option: Mission Control from Mercury to Apollo 13 and Beyond*. New York: Simon & Shuster, Inc.

Maltin, L., ed. 2002. *Leonard Maltin's Movie & Video Guide, 2003 Edition*. New York: SIGNET.

Martin, M., and Porter, M., eds. 2002. *Video & DVD Guide 2003*. New York: Ballantine Books.

Mooij, J. J. A. 1976. *A Study of Metaphor: On the Nature of Metaphorical Expressions, with Special References to their Reference*. Amsterdam: North-Holland Publishing Co.

Proctor II, R. F., and Adler, R. B. 1991. Teaching Interpersonal Communication With Feature Films. *Communication Education* 40: 393–400.

Seuss, Dr., *Horton Hears a Who!* New York: Random House, 1976.

Stadler, H. A. 1990. Film As Experience: Phenomenological Concepts in Cinema and Television Studies. *Quarterly Review of Film and Video* 12: 37–50.

Test, G. A. 1991. *Satire: Spirit and Art*. Tampa, FL: University of South Florida Press.

Wolensky, R. P., ed. 1982. *Using Films in Sociology Courses: Guidelines and Reviews*. Washington, DC: American Sociological Association.

Zorn, T. F. 1991. Willy Loman's Lesson: Teaching Identity Management with *Death of a Salesman*. *Communication Education* 40: 219–224.

I n d e x

Note: This index separately notes film directors and book authors. It does not separately note actresses and actors. The index also calls out all non-English language films.